MICROSOFT COPILOT USER GUIDE

Essential user manual for Harnessing the Power of Advanced Features to Revolutionize Your Workflow and Boost Productivity

By

Alicia Morgan

INTRODUCTION

Welcome to the "Microsoft Copilot User Guide," your comprehensive manual to navigating and mastering the world of artificial intelligence assistance. This guide is not just a collection of instructions; it's a gateway to enhancing your digital interactions and productivity through the innovative capabilities of Microsoft Copilot.

Imagine a tool that understands your needs, adapts to your style, and empowers you to achieve more with less effort. That's the essence of Microsoft Copilot. Whether you're drafting emails, coding an application, or simply seeking information, Copilot is designed to be your reliable partner, transforming the way you work and interact with technology.

A Transformation Story of Alex

Let me share with you the story of Alex, a freelance graphic designer with a passion for photography. Alex's journey with Microsoft Copilot began out of curiosity but quickly turned into a tale of transformation. Initially overwhelmed by the demands of managing multiple projects, Alex found solace in the pages of this very guide.

By following the step-by-step instructions, Alex learned to delegate routine tasks to Copilot, from scheduling appointments to searching for design inspiration. But the real game-changer was when Alex discovered Copilot's ability to assist with photo editing workflows. Using natural language, Alex could instruct Copilot to perform complex adjustments in Lightroom Photoshop, a task that once consumed hours of meticulous work.

As Alex became more proficient, the guide's advanced sections unveiled deeper functionalities. Copilot's code generation feature allowed Alex to customize a website portfolio with ease, something that previously seemed daunting. The guide's tips and tricks section revealed shortcuts and hidden features, further streamlining Alex's creative process.

From Beginner to Pro

This guide is structured to cater to both beginners and seasoned users. It starts with the basics, ensuring a solid foundation, and gradually progresses to more sophisticated uses. By the end, you'll not only be proficient in the standard features but also adept at leveraging Copilot's full potential.

The real-life story of Alex is a testament to the transformative power of this guide. It's proof that with the right resource, anyone can ascend from novice to expert. As you turn each page, you'll find yourself equipped with the knowledge and confidence to harness Copilot's capabilities fully.

Remember, Microsoft Copilot is more than just a tool; it's a companion in your digital journey. And this guide is your roadmap to unlocking its possibilities. So embark on this adventure with an open mind, and you'll soon find yourself moving from beginner to pro in using Microsoft Copilot.

What is Microsoft Copilot?

Microsoft Copilot is an advanced AI tool designed to be your everyday digital companion, enhancing your productivity and creativity across a multitude of tasks. It's a versatile assistant that leverages the power of generative AI to help you find information, create content, and streamline your workflow with unprecedented efficiency.

The Essence of Copilot

At its core, Microsoft Copilot is built upon a sophisticated language model capable of understanding and generating human-like text. This enables it to perform a wide range of functions, from simple tasks like setting reminders to complex ones such as coding assistance and language translation. It's an evolution of AI assistance, aiming to be more intuitive and integrated into your daily life than ever before.

Capabilities and Features

Information at Your Fingertips: Whether you're looking for quick facts, detailed research, or anything in between, Copilot can provide accurate information swiftly1.

Content Creation: Need to draft an email, write a report, or come up with creative writing? Copilot can generate text based on your prompts, saving you time and effort2.

Design and Media: With the ability to create images from text descriptions, Copilot can aid in graphic design, making it a valuable tool for artists and designers2.

Coding Made Easy: Copilot isn't just for non-technical users; it can write code in various programming languages, making it a boon for developers3.

1.Generative AI at Your Service

At the heart of Copilot lies a sophisticated language model powered by generative AI. This model has been meticulously trained to comprehend natural language and generate contextually relevant responses. Whether you're drafting an email, writing code, or creating content, Copilot collaborates with you, making your tasks more efficient and enjoyable.

2. Your Personal AI Companion

Copilot seamlessly integrates into your Microsoft 365 apps, documents, and meetings. Here are some key features:

Copilot in Word: Bring your ideas to life by quickly creating drafts on any topic. Copilot assists you in crafting well-structured content, whether it's a report, an essay, or a blog post.

Copilot in Excel: Simplify data analysis and visualization. Copilot helps you with formulas, charts, and data manipulation.

Copilot in PowerPoint: Elevate your presentations. Copilot suggests impactful phrases, slide layouts, and design elements.

Copilot in Teams: Enhance collaboration during meetings. Copilot provides real-time assistance, turning discussions into actionable outcomes.

3. From Novice to Pro: Your Journey with Copilot

Copilot caters to users of all levels:

Beginners: If you're new to Copilot, fear not! Start with basic commands and gradually explore its capabilities. Copilot will guide you through the essentials.

Intermediate Users: Dive deeper into advanced features. Learn how to optimize code, create stunning visuals, and streamline your workflow.

Experts: Copilot's hidden gems await you. Discover shortcuts, tips, and personalized settings. Become a Copilot virtuoso.

The Evolution of AI Assistants

The journey of AI assistants is a fascinating tale of technological advancement and human ingenuity. From their inception as simple programmed responses to becoming an integral part of our daily lives, AI assistants have undergone a remarkable transformation. This evolution has been shaped by breakthroughs in machine learning, natural language processing, and user interface design, leading to more intuitive and context-aware systems capable of anticipating user needs and providing personalized support[4].

The Dawn of AI Assistants

The story begins in the late 1960s with the development of the first virtual assistants. These early chatbots, like ELIZA developed in 1966, laid the groundwork for future innovations[3]. They were rudimentary by today's standards, but they sparked the imagination of what could be possible.

The Rise of Personal Assistants

Fast forward to the early 21st century, and we witnessed the emergence of voice-activated AI assistants like Siri and Alexa. These pioneers offered basic information retrieval and task execution, laying the foundation for the sophisticated systems we see today.

The Era of Contextual Understanding

Today's AI personal assistants have evolved to understand context, recognize user preferences, and engage in natural, dynamic conversations. They are not just reactive but proactive, capable of completing entire flows of tasks on your behalf.

The Future of AI Assistants

As we look toward the horizon, the evolution of AI virtual assistants is poised to accelerate further. With advancements in AI technologies, they are expected to become even more integrated into our lives, eliminating mundane tasks and helping us become more productive.

How to use this Guide for better result

Embarking on the journey with Microsoft Copilot can be both exciting and daunting. This guide is your compass, designed to navigate you through the functionalities and possibilities that Copilot offers. Here's how this guide can help you harness the full potential of Microsoft Copilot:

1. Understanding the Basics

- Product Introduction: Gain an overview of Microsoft Copilot, its purpose, and what you can achieve with it[1].

- Installation and Setup: Step-by-step instructions to get Copilot up and running smoothly in your digital environment.

2. Mastering Daily Operations

- Everyday Commands: Learn the essential commands that will make your daily interactions with Copilot efficient and productive[1].

- Task Management: Discover how to manage your tasks, set reminders, and keep your schedule organized with Copilot's assistance.

3. Leveraging Advanced Features

- Content Creation: Unleash your creativity with Copilot's content generation capabilities, from writing emails to creating stories[1].

- Coding Assistance: Dive into the world of coding with Copilot's guidance, whether you're a beginner or an experienced developer.

4. Enhancing Productivity

- Maximizing Efficiency: Tips and tricks to get the most out of Copilot, saving you time and effort on various tasks[1].

- Troubleshooting: Learn how to solve common challenges and errors with Copilot, ensuring a smooth experience[1].

5. Expanding Knowledge

- FAQs: A comprehensive list of frequently asked questions to help you resolve doubts and learn more about Copilot's features.

- Glossary: Understand the jargon and technical terms related to Copilot and AI assistants.

6. Customizing Your Experience

- Personalization: Tailor Copilot to your needs and preferences for a more personalized experience.

- Integration: Connect Copilot with other apps and services to expand its functionality and adapt it to your workflow.

7. Preparing for the Future

- Staying Informed: Keep up with the latest developments in AI and how they might impact the future of digital assistants like Copilot.

- Ethical Considerations: Explore the ethical dimensions of using AI assistants and how to use Copilot responsibly.

This guide is not just a manual; it's a resource that grows with you as you explore the depths of what Microsoft Copilot can do. Whether you're looking to streamline your work, enhance your creativity, or simply make your day-to-day tasks easier, this guide is the key to unlocking a new level of digital proficiency. Let's embark on this journey together, and transform the way you interact with technology.

Chapter 2: Getting Started with Microsoft Copilot

Setting Up Your Copilot

Setting up Microsoft Copilot is your first step towards unlocking a world of productivity and creativity. This section will guide you through the process of getting Copilot ready to assist you in your daily tasks and projects. Here's how to set up your Copilot:

1. Prerequisites

Before you begin, ensure you have the following:

- A compatible subscription plan for Microsoft Copilot.

- One of the prerequisite licenses such as Microsoft 365 E5, E3, F1, F3, Office 365 E1, E3, E5, or others.

- Microsoft 365 Apps desktop applications like Word, Excel, PowerPoint, Outlook, and Teams installed.

2. Optimizing for Search

Optimize your environment for search to ensure Copilot can effectively retrieve and utilize data from your Microsoft Graph and Microsoft 365 Apps.

3. Provision Copilot Licenses

Purchase and assign the necessary Copilot licenses through the Microsoft 365 admin center, Microsoft partners, or your Microsoft account team.

4. OneDrive Account

Set up a OneDrive account, which is essential for saving and sharing files with Copilot.

5. Outlook Integration

For seamless integration with Outlook, use the new Outlook (Windows, Mac, Web, Mobile). Copilot supports classic Outlook as well, but the new version is recommended.

6. Microsoft Teams

To use Copilot with Microsoft Teams, ensure you have the Teams desktop client or access to the web client[1].

7. Deployment Guide

Follow the Deployment guide for Microsoft 365 Apps to start the implementation process.

8. Announce Copilot

Inform your users about Copilot and its features, ensuring they are aware of the new tool at their disposal.

By following these steps, you'll have Microsoft Copilot set up and ready to enhance your productivity and creativity across Microsoft 365 Apps. Whether you're drafting documents, analyzing data, or managing communications, Copilot is designed to be a versatile and intelligent assistant that adapts to your needs.

Navigating the Interface

In the world of Microsoft Copilot, navigating the interface is as intuitive as conversing with a friend. This section will guide you through the various aspects of Copilot's interface, ensuring you can make the most of this powerful tool with ease.

1. Accessing Copilot

- Through the Website: You can access Copilot by visiting the official website and logging in with your Microsoft account[4].

- Sidebar Integration: Copilot can also be accessed as a sidebar on your desktop, providing easy access via the Taskbar or using the shortcut key Windows + C.

- Microsoft Edge Browser: For those who prefer browsing, Copilot is available through the Microsoft Edge browser, offering a seamless experience.

2. Interface Overview

- Taskbar Icon: Look for the Copilot icon on your taskbar. Clicking it will launch Copilot as a sidebar on the right edge of your screen[7].

- Sidebar Layout: The sidebar layout is designed to not overlap with your desktop content, allowing you to interact with Copilot while working on other tasks[7].

3. Navigating Within Microsoft 365 Apps

- Word, Excel, PowerPoint: Copilot is integrated into Microsoft 365 apps like Word, Excel, and PowerPoint, where it assists with drafting, data analysis, and presentation design.

- Outlook: In Outlook, Copilot helps manage emails and schedules, accessible through a dedicated pane within the application.

4. Using Copilot Effectively

- Prompts: Learn to optimize your prompts for better results. Clear and specific prompts will yield more accurate and helpful responses from Copilot.

Personal Information: Be mindful of safeguarding personal information when interacting with Copilot. Ensure that sensitive data is not inadvertently shared.

5. Customization and Preferences

- Settings: Customize your Copilot experience through the settings menu, where you can adjust preferences and manage how Copilot interacts with your data.

- Feedback Loop: Use the feedback feature to report any issues or suggest improvements, helping to refine the Copilot experience over time.

6. Exploring Features

- Discoverability: Explore the full potential of Copilot by trying out different features and commands. The interface is designed to be user-friendly and encourages exploration[1].

- Help and Support: Access help and support directly from the interface. Copilot provides guidance and tutorials to help you understand its capabilities.

By familiarizing yourself with the Copilot interface and its navigation, you'll be well on your way to leveraging the full power of AI to enhance your productivity and creativity. Whether you're a first-time user or looking to deepen your understanding, this guide will ensure you're equipped to navigate Copilot's interface with confidence.

Customizing Your Experience

Microsoft Copilot is not just a tool; it's an extension of your digital self. Customizing your experience with Copilot is key to making it work for you in the most efficient way possible. Here's how you can tailor Copilot to fit your unique needs and preferences:

1. Personalization

- User Preferences: Set your language preferences, preferred content types, and interaction styles to make Copilot truly yours.

- Learning Your Style: Copilot can learn from your writing style and preferences to offer suggestions that are in line with your tone and manner.

2. Custom Copilots with Copilot Studio

- Build Your Own: Use Copilot Studio to create custom Copilots tailored to specific roles, functions, or business processes.

- Integrate with Your Data: Connect Copilot with your organization's data, from SharePoint sites to custom backends, for a more informed assistant.

3. Extensions and Add-Ons

- Copilot Extensions: Enhance your Copilot experience by adding unique skills and connecting with external data and systems.

- Developer Tools:Utilize Microsoft Teams Toolkit for Visual Studio Code to build Copilot extensions tailored to your workflow.

4. Workflow Optimization

- Automate Tasks: Set up Copilot to automate repetitive tasks, from scheduling to data entry, freeing up your time for more important work.

- Custom Skills: Teach Copilot custom skills relevant to your industry or profession for a more specialized assistant.

5. Accessibility and Inclusivity

- Accessibility Settings: Adjust text size, contrast, and other settings to ensure Copilot is accessible to all users.

- Inclusive Language: Copilot can be set to use inclusive language, promoting a respectful and welcoming environment.

6. Feedback and Evolution

- Continuous Feedback: Provide feedback on your experience to help Copilot evolve and better suit your needs over time[1].

- Community Contributions: Engage with the Copilot community to share customizations and learn from others' experiences.

Chapter 3: Basic Commands and Functions

Everyday Commands

Mastering the everyday commands of Microsoft Copilot is like learning the secret handshake to a more productive digital life. These commands are the building blocks that will help you navigate through your tasks with ease and efficiency. Here's a comprehensive look at the everyday commands you can use with Copilot:

1. Basic Navigation and Operations

Open Applications: Use commands like "Open [app name]" to launch applications on your device1.

System Settings: Adjust settings such as "Turn on dark mode" or "Change wallpaper" with simple instructions.

Device Control: Manage your device's functions like Bluetooth, volume, and network connections with commands like "Mute volume" or "Connect to a network".

2. Content Creation and Editing

Writing Assistance: Draft emails, reports, or creative content by instructing Copilot with prompts like "Draft an email regarding [topic]" keeping the tone "[formal/friendly]".

Editing Suggestions: Improve your documents by asking Copilot to "Make the third paragraph more concise" or "Change the tone of the document to be more casual".

3. Data Analysis and Management

Excel Operations: Perform data analysis, create charts, and automate Excel tasks with commands like "Summarize this data set" or "Create a pivot table for these sales figures".

File Management: Organize your files and documents with commands such as "Find reference in a file" or "Summarize a document".

4. Communication and Scheduling

Email Management: Compose and manage emails efficiently with prompts like "Draft an email to the team about the project update"4.

Meeting Summaries: Catch up on meetings or prepare for upcoming ones with commands like "Summarize the last team meeting" or "Prepare an agenda for tomorrow's meeting".

5. Web and Search Operations

Internet Browsing: In the Edge browser, use Copilot to organize tabs or perform searches with commands like "Organize my tabs" or "Search for the latest AI research papers".

Content Summarization: Summarize web pages or articles by asking Copilot to "Summarize this article for me".

6. Learning and Development

Skill Enhancement: Learn new skills or get explanations on topics with prompts like "Explain the concept of machine learning" or "Teach me how to write a haiku".

Language Translation: Translate text or learn phrases in different languages with commands like "Translate 'Hello, how are you?' to Spanish".

7. Entertainment and Leisure

Creative Requests: Ask Copilot to "Tell me a joke" or "Suggest a movie for movie night".

Travel Planning: Plan your vacations or outings with prompts like "Plan a vacation to Japan for two weeks".

By familiarizing yourself with these everyday commands, you'll be able to interact with Microsoft Copilot more naturally and effectively. Whether you're looking to streamline your workflow, enhance your creativity, or simply make your day-to-day tasks easier, these commands are your stepping stones to a more empowered digital experience with Copilot.

Managing Tasks and Reminders

Efficiently managing tasks and reminders is crucial for staying organized and productive. Microsoft Copilot simplifies this process by integrating with your Microsoft 365 applications, allowing you to create, track, and manage your tasks with ease. Here's a detailed explanation of how you can use Copilot to manage your tasks and reminders:

1. Creating a To-Do List

OneNote Integration: Use Copilot within OneNote to extract a to-do list from your meeting notes or brainstorming sessions.

Task Extraction: Simply enter a command like "Extract a to-do list from these notes" in the Copilot pane, and it will generate a list of tasks for you.

2. Setting Reminders

Outlook Synchronization: Set reminders for your tasks directly in Outlook. Copilot can help you manage and triage your emails and time more efficiently, providing personalized suggestions and insights.

Voice Commands: Use voice commands to set reminders for specific tasks or deadlines. For example, "Remind me to follow up on the project proposal next Monday at 10 AM."

3. Tracking Progress

Microsoft Loop Integration: Assign and track tasks with due dates, reminders, and dependencies. Access your content from any device, online or offline, and integrate with other Microsoft 365 apps and services.

Visual Tracking: Utilize Copilot's capabilities to create visual representations of your task progress, such as charts or graphs.

4. Automating Follow-Ups

Email Follow-Ups: After meetings, use Copilot to generate follow-up emails sorted by action items, pending issues, and next steps, ensuring everyone stays on track.

Meeting Summaries: Create instant meeting summaries with tasks and auto-generate follow-ups for efficient team collaboration.

5. Prioritizing Tasks

Smart Prioritization: Copilot can help you prioritize tasks based on urgency, deadlines, or your personal preferences.

Custom Filters: Set up custom filters to view tasks by project, due date, or other criteria.

6. Integration with Daily Workflow

Seamless Workflow: Integrate task management into your daily workflow with Copilot's assistance across various Microsoft 365 apps.

Cross-Application Sync: Ensure that your tasks and reminders are synced across all your devices and applications for a unified view.

By leveraging Microsoft Copilot for managing tasks and reminders, you can streamline your workflow, reduce the cognitive load of keeping track of numerous tasks, and focus on what truly matters.

Whether you're a project manager coordinating a team or an individual juggling multiple responsibilities, Copilot's task management features are designed to keep you organized and ahead of the curve.

Searching the Web

In the digital age, the ability to search the web effectively is as essential as knowing how to read and write. With the vast expanse of information available online, knowing how to find exactly what you're looking for can save you time and enhance your productivity. Here's a comprehensive guide on how to harness the power of search engines to navigate the sea of data on the internet:

1. Understanding Search Engines

What is a Search Engine?: A search engine is a software system designed to carry out web searches. It sifts through the internet's vast resources to present you with information relevant to your query.

Popular Search Engines: While Google remains the most widely used search engine, others like Bing, DuckDuckGo, and Yandex offer unique features and privacy options.

2. Crafting Effective Queries

Keywords: Identify the main concepts of your information need and use them as keywords in your search.

Phrase Searches: Use quotation marks to search for exact phrases to get more precise results.

Boolean Operators: Utilize operators like AND, OR, and NOT to refine your search results.

3. Refining Your Search

Advanced Search Options: Most search engines offer advanced search options that allow you to narrow down results by language, region, date, and more.

Using Filters: Apply filters to your search results to quickly find the type of content you're looking for, such as images, videos, or news articles.

4. Evaluating Sources

Relevance: Check if the information directly addresses your query.

Authority: Consider the source's credibility and expertise on the topic.

Currency: Look for the most up-to-date information, especially if the topic is time-sensitive.

5. Search Engine Features

Image and Video Search: Use search engines' specialized features to find media related to your query.

Voice Search: Modern search engines often support voice queries, making it easier to search without typing.

6. Privacy Considerations

Data Collection: Be aware that some search engines collect data about your searches which can be used for targeted advertising.

Private Browsing: Use privacy-focused search engines or private browsing modes to minimize data collection.

7. Staying Informed

Search Engine Updates: Keep up with changes and updates to search engines, as they constantly evolve to provide better results and new features.

Learning Resources: Explore tutorials and guides to improve your web searching skills and stay informed about best practices.

By mastering the art of searching the web, you'll be able to find reliable information quickly and efficiently. Whether you're conducting academic research, looking for the latest news, or simply satisfying your curiosity, these tips will help you navigate the web like a pro. Remember, the key to effective searching is not just in asking but in asking the right way.

Chapter 4: Advanced Features

Deep Dives into Creative Writing

Creative writing is an art form that allows individuals to express themselves through the written word in a way that goes beyond the bounds of conventional professional, journalistic, academic, or technical forms of literature. It's a craft that encompasses a variety of genres and styles, including poetry, fiction, playwriting, and non-fiction. A deep dive into creative writing involves immersing oneself in the nuances of storytelling, character development, world-building, and the exploration of themes and emotions that resonate with readers.

The Journey of Creative Exploration

Self-Discovery: Through creative writing, writers often embark on a journey of self-discovery, learning about their own values, beliefs, and experiences as they weave them into their narratives[1].

Skill Enhancement: As writers delve deeper, they refine their skills, experimenting with different narrative techniques, points of view, and stylistic choices.

Techniques and Tools

Writing Prompts: Utilizing writing prompts can spark creativity, offering new perspectives and challenging writers to think outside the box1.

Workshops and Critique: Engaging in workshops and peer critiques provides valuable feedback, helping writers to hone their craft and improve their work.

The Creative Process

Drafting and Revision: The process of writing and revising is fundamental to creative writing. It's a cycle of creation and refinement, seeking to perfect the rhythm, flow, and impact of the story.

Character and Plot Development: Developing compelling characters and intriguing plots are central to storytelling, requiring a deep understanding of human nature and narrative structure.

The Writer's Voice

Unique Voice: Every writer has a unique voice, and a deep dive into creative writing helps to cultivate that distinctiveness, making their work stand out.

Authenticity: Authenticity is key in creative writing. It's about being true to one's style and the story being told, which connects with readers on a deeper level.

The Impact of Creative Writing

Cultural and Social Influence: Creative writing has the power to influence culture and society, often reflecting and challenging societal norms and issues.

Personal and Emotional Connection: Stories can evoke a range of emotions, creating a personal connection between the writer and the reader1.

Code Generation and Assistance

The landscape of software development is continually evolving, and one of the most significant advancements in recent years has been the integration of AI in code generation and assistance. This technology has revolutionized the way developers write, debug, and maintain code, making the process more efficient and less error-prone.

The Advent of AI in Coding

AI-Powered Code Generators: Tools like GitHub Copilot have emerged, offering predictive code generation that suggests entire lines or blocks of code as you type, adapting to your coding style over time.

Multilingual Support: These tools are trained on a multitude of public code repositories, enabling them to understand and assist with a vast range of programming languages.

Enhancing Developer Productivity

Automating Routine Tasks: AI assists in automating repetitive coding tasks, allowing developers to focus on more complex and creative aspects of software development.

Error Detection and Correction: AI coding assistants can identify bugs and errors in real-time, suggesting fixes before the code is even run.

Streamlining the Development Process

Code Refactoring: AI tools can help clean up code, making it more readable and maintainable by generating docstrings, adding comments, and formatting the code.

Natural Language Queries: Developers can interact with AI assistants using natural language, making it easier to generate complex code or understand code functionality.

Security and Code Quality

Vulnerability Detection: AI code assistants can scan for security vulnerabilities, providing suggestions for how to fix them, thus enhancing the security of the codebase.

Code Optimization: AI can suggest optimizations to improve code quality and performance, ensuring that the code is not only functional but also efficient.

The Future of Code Generation

Continuous Learning: As AI code generators learn from each developer's unique coding style, the suggestions become more personalized and accurate, leading to a more intuitive coding experience.

Collaborative Coding: AI code assistants are paving the way for a more collaborative coding environment, where the tool acts as a virtual pair programmer, contributing to the codebase alongside human developers.

Language Translation Capabilities

The ability to communicate across languages is a cornerstone of our global society. Language translation capabilities have evolved significantly with the advent of technology, particularly through the development of artificial intelligence (AI). Here's an overview of the current state and potential of language translation capabilities:

1. Real-Time Translation

Instant Communication: AI-powered services provide real-time translation for text and speech, enabling instant communication across different languages.

Multilingual Conversational Agents: These agents can facilitate conversations in multiple languages, making them invaluable for customer service and international relations.

2. Machine Translation Engines

Broad Language Coverage: Modern translation engines can handle over 100 languages, offering broad accessibility and inclusivity.

Customizable Translations: AI translation services allow for the creation of custom models to handle domain-specific terminology, ensuring accuracy in specialized fields.

3. Integration and Accessibility

API Access: Translation capabilities can be integrated into apps and solutions with a single REST API call, extending the reach of applications.

Flexible Programming: Support for various programming languages, including Python, C#, Java, JavaScript, and Go, makes it easier for developers to incorporate translation features into their projects.

4. Quality and Reliability

Production-Ready: The translation engines used are tested at scale, powering translations across major products and services, ensuring reliability and quality.

Security: Built-in security measures ensure that data remains private, with text input not being logged during translation.

5. The Future of Translation

AI Advancements: As AI continues to advance, the accuracy and speed of translations are expected to improve, making machine translation increasingly competitive with human translators.

Ethical Considerations: The development of AI translation raises questions about the future of human translators and the importance of maintaining cultural nuances in translation.

6. Challenges and Opportunities

Cultural Nuances: While AI has made great strides, capturing the subtleties of culture and context remains a challenge.

Continuous Learning: AI systems learn from vast amounts of data, improving over time to provide more accurate and contextually relevant translations.

Chapter 5: Tips and Tricks

Maximizing Productivity with Copilot

In the fast-paced digital world, maximizing productivity is not just about working harder but working smarter. Microsoft Copilot is designed to enhance your efficiency and streamline your workflow. Here's a comprehensive guide to leveraging Copilot for peak productivity:

1. Understanding Copilot's Capabilities

AI-Powered Efficiency: Recognize the full spectrum of Copilot's AI-powered capabilities, from content creation to data analysis.

Task Automation: Utilize Copilot to automate routine tasks, freeing up your time for more complex and creative endeavors.

2. Integrating Copilot into Your Workflow

Seamless Integration: Embed Copilot into your daily routine by integrating it with Microsoft 365 apps for a unified productivity experience.

Cross-Platform Use: Access Copilot across various platforms, ensuring that your productivity tools are always at your fingertips.

3. Customizing Copilot for Personal Use

Personal Preferences: Tailor Copilot's settings to align with your personal work style and preferences for a more intuitive experience.

Learning and Adapting: Teach Copilot your unique workflow patterns so it can better anticipate your needs and streamline your processes.

4. Advanced Features for Professionals

Professional Tools: Dive into Copilot's advanced features, such as code assistance for developers and design tools for creatives.

Data Handling: Leverage Copilot's ability to handle large datasets, perform complex calculations, and generate visual representations.

5. Communication and Collaboration

Enhanced Communication: Use Copilot to draft emails, prepare reports, and create presentations that communicate your ideas effectively.

Collaborative Projects: Facilitate teamwork by sharing Copilot-generated documents and insights, ensuring everyone is on the same page.

6. Time Management and Scheduling

Smart Scheduling: Employ Copilot to manage your calendar, set reminders, and prioritize tasks based on deadlines and importance.

Meeting Efficiency: Prepare for meetings with Copilot's summarization features and follow-up with action items and notes.

7. Learning and Development

Continuous Learning: Stay ahead of the curve by using Copilot as a learning tool to acquire new skills and knowledge.

Skill Enhancement: Improve your proficiency in various applications and software through Copilot's guided tutorials and explanations.

8. Health and Well-Being

Work-Life Balance: Maintain a healthy work-life balance by setting boundaries and using Copilot to manage workloads efficiently.

Mindfulness and Breaks: Schedule regular breaks and mindfulness sessions with Copilot to stay focused and avoid burnout.

9. Custom Scripts and Macros

Automation Scripts: Create custom scripts and macros with Copilot's assistance to automate repetitive tasks across applications.

Efficiency Hacks: Discover and implement Copilot-suggested efficiency hacks to speed up your workflow.

10. Feedback and Evolution

User Feedback: Provide feedback on your experience with Copilot to help it evolve and better suit your productivity needs.

Community Engagement: Engage with the Copilot user community to exchange tips and best practices for maximizing productivity.

If you follow this guide very well, you'll be able to transform the way you work, making the most of your time and resources. Microsoft Copilot is not just a tool; it's your partner in productivity, helping you achieve your goals with greater ease and efficiency. Embrace the power of AI and watch your productivity soar!

Hidden Features and Easter Eggs with Copilot

Uncovering the hidden features and Easter eggs within Microsoft Copilot can be a delightful experience, adding an element of surprise and fun to your daily interactions with the AI. Here's a comprehensive and detailed content guide to some of the lesser-known functionalities and whimsical secrets embedded in Copilot:

1. The Playful Side of Copilot

Easter Eggs: Discover the fun side of Copilot with hidden commands that trigger amusing responses or actions.

Secret Commands: Learn about secret commands that unlock playful interactions or display hidden messages from the developers1.

2. Customization Secrets

Personalization Tricks: Dive into advanced customization options that are not immediately apparent, allowing for a more personalized experience1.

Theme Changes: Explore how to change themes and visual aspects of Copilot in unexpected ways.

3. Hidden Functionalities

Undocumented Features: Unearth functionalities that are not widely documented but can enhance your productivity or provide new ways to use Copilot1.

AI Navigation Assistant: Find out about the AI Navigation Assistant, a hidden feature that helps you navigate complex software environments.

4. AI Reading Assistant

Reading Modes: Discover the AI Reading Assistant, a feature that can help you digest large amounts of text through summarization and key point extraction.

Learning Tools: Utilize hidden learning tools that can assist with language learning or understanding complex topics.

5. Free AI Image Creation

Image Generation: Learn about the hidden ability of Copilot to generate images based on textual descriptions, adding a visual dimension to your creative projects.

6. GPT-4 Accessibility

Advanced Language Model: Gain access to the advanced capabilities of GPT-4, which may include nuanced language understanding and generation.

7. Entertainment and Games

Built-in Games: Find built-in games and challenges within Copilot that can provide a quick mental break or a bit of entertainment during your workday.

8. Surprise Interactions

Random Surprises: Encounter random surprises and interactions that make each session with Copilot unique and engaging.

9. Developer Homages

Tributes to Developers: Discover tributes and homages to the developers and creators of Copilot, hidden within the interface or commands.

10. Community Discoveries

User-Found Secrets: Participate in the community of Copilot users who share their discoveries of hidden features and Easter eggs.

Troubleshooting Common Issues

Troubleshooting common issues with Microsoft Copilot involves a systematic approach to identify and resolve problems that may arise during its use. Here's a detailed explanation of how to address some of the typical challenges users might encounter:

1. Understanding Copilot's Functionality

Function Overview: Familiarize yourself with Copilot's range of functions to better understand expected behaviors and performance.

Role in Daily Tasks: Recognize how Copilot integrates with various Microsoft applications to assist in tasks like drafting documents and data analysis.

2. Common Problems and Solutions

Connectivity Issues: If Copilot is not connecting, check your internet connection, firewall settings, and ensure that Copilot services are operational.

Performance Hiccups: For lag or performance issues, ensure your system meets the minimum requirements and that you have the latest updates installed.

3. Error Messages

Deciphering Errors: Understand the error codes or messages provided by Copilot to determine the nature of the problem.

Knowledge Base: Use Microsoft's knowledge base or community forums to find solutions to known error messages.

4. Update and Maintenance

Regular Updates: Keep Copilot and your Microsoft 365 apps updated to the latest version to prevent compatibility issues.

System Maintenance: Perform regular system maintenance, such as clearing cache and restarting your device, to keep Copilot running smoothly.

5. Advanced Troubleshooting

Registry Edits: For advanced users, making changes in the Registry Editor can resolve certain issues, but this should be done with caution and typically as a last resort.

Reinstallation: If problems persist, consider reinstalling Copilot and related applications.

6. Seeking Support

Microsoft Support: Reach out to Microsoft Support for assistance with unresolved issues.

Community Assistance: Engage with the Copilot user community for shared experiences and troubleshooting tips.

7. Preventive Measures

Best Practices: Follow best practices for using Copilot, such as regularly saving work and avoiding the input of sensitive information.

Training and Resources: Utilize training resources to better understand how to use Copilot effectively and prevent common mistakes.

Chapter 6: Safety and Privacy

Understanding Copilot's Safety Protocols

Ensuring the safety and security of users is a top priority for Microsoft Copilot. The AI is designed with multiple layers of safety protocols to protect users and their data. Here's a detailed look at the safety measures in place:

1. Data Privacy and Security

Secure Data Handling: Copilot adheres to strict data privacy policies, ensuring that user data is handled securely and confidentially1.

Compliance with Regulations: It complies with international data protection regulations, including GDPR, to safeguard user information.

2. Ethical AI Practices

Bias Mitigation: Efforts are made to mitigate biases in AI responses, promoting fairness and inclusivity.

Responsible AI Use: Guidelines for responsible AI use are in place to prevent misuse and ensure ethical interactions.

3. Content Filtering

Inappropriate Content Block: Copilot has mechanisms to block the generation or display of inappropriate content.

Contextual Awareness: The AI is contextually aware, filtering out unwanted results and providing high-quality, relevant responses3.

4. User Safety Features

Safety Warnings: Copilot provides clear warnings and disclaimers when necessary, especially when dealing with sensitive topics2.

User Control: Users have control over their interactions with Copilot and can customize settings for a safer experience.

5. Intellectual Property Protection

Infringement Prevention: Measures are in place to prevent the infringement of intellectual property, protecting both users and third parties.

Creative Content Generation: While Copilot can generate creative content, it adheres to safety guidelines to ensure originality and respect for copyright laws.

6. Continuous Improvement

Feedback Loop: A feedback loop allows users to report concerns or issues, which are used to improve Copilot's safety features.

Regular Updates: Copilot undergoes regular updates to enhance its safety protocols and address emerging security challenges.

7. Training and Awareness

User Education: Resources are available to educate users on safe and responsible use of Copilot.

Community Engagement: The Copilot community plays a role in maintaining a safe environment by sharing best practices and reporting vulnerabilities.

By understanding these safety protocols, users can feel confident in their interactions with Microsoft Copilot. The AI is built to be a secure, reliable, and ethical assistant that respects user privacy and promotes a safe digital environment.

Ensuring Your Data Privacy

In an era where data breaches are not uncommon, ensuring your data privacy is more crucial than ever. Data privacy refers to the practice of protecting personal, private, or sensitive information, ensuring it's collected with proper consent, kept secure, and used only for authorized purposes, while respecting both individual rights and existing regulations1. Here's how you can safeguard your digital privacy:

1. Strong Passwords and Authentication

Create Strong, Unique Passwords: Use complex passwords that are difficult to guess and unique for each account.

Two-Factor Authentication: Add an extra layer of security by enabling two-factor authentication wherever possible.

2. Software and App Updates

Regular Updates: Keep your software and apps updated to protect against the latest security vulnerabilities.

3. Mindful Sharing

Be Cautious with Sharing: Think twice before sharing personal information online and be aware of where and to whom you are giving this information.

4. Understanding Permissions

Read Permissions and Pop-Ups: Always read the permissions and pop-up messages before accepting them to understand what data you are agreeing to share.

5. Monitoring Accounts

Regular Account Checks: Monitor your personal accounts for any unusual activity that could indicate a breach.

6. Privacy Settings

Adjust Privacy Settings: Make use of the privacy settings on social media and other online platforms to control who can see your information.

7. Avoiding Personal Info in AI Apps

Limit Personal Info: Be cautious about the amount of personal information you provide to AI applications.

8. Cookie Management

Manage Cookies: Reject browser cookies whenever possible or use browsers that avoid cross-site tracking, like DuckDuckGo, Brave, or Firefox.

9. Advocacy for Data Protection

Support Federal Data Protections: Advocate for stronger data protection laws at the federal level to ensure comprehensive privacy rights.

By taking these steps, you can significantly enhance the privacy and security of your data. While no system is entirely foolproof, being proactive about your digital privacy can help mitigate risks and protect your personal information in the digital world.

Best Practices for Secure Usage

In the digital realm, secure usage practices are essential to protect against cyber threats and ensure the integrity of your data. Below is a comprehensive and detailed guide to best practices for secure usage:

1. Understanding Security Fundamentals

Security Awareness: Stay informed about the latest cybersecurity threats and trends.

Risk Assessment: Regularly assess your digital assets for vulnerabilities and potential risks.

2. Strong Authentication Measures

Complex Passwords: Create strong, unique passwords for all accounts and change them periodically.

Multi-Factor Authentication (MFA): Enable MFA wherever possible to add an extra layer of security.

3. Regular Software Updates

Update Promptly: Keep your operating system, applications, and security software up to date to patch vulnerabilities.

4. Safe Browsing Habits

Suspicious Links: Think before you click on links, especially those from unknown sources.

Secure Connections: Use secure, encrypted connections like HTTPS, and consider using a VPN for additional privacy.

5. Data Encryption

Encrypt Sensitive Data: Use encryption for sensitive files, both in transit and at rest, to prevent unauthorized access.

6. Network Security

Firewalls: Utilize firewalls to block unauthorized access to your network and devices.

Secure Wi-Fi: Ensure your Wi-Fi network is secure, using strong encryption like WPA.

7. Email Security

Phishing Awareness: Be vigilant about phishing attempts and verify the authenticity of emails before responding.

Email Encryption: Encrypt sensitive emails to protect the information they contain.

8. Device Security

Physical Security: Keep your devices physically secure to prevent theft or unauthorized access1.

Remote Wipe: Set up the ability to remotely wipe data from your devices in case they are lost or stolen.

9. Backup and Recovery

Regular Backups: Back up your data regularly to multiple locations, including cloud services and external drives.

Disaster Recovery Plan: Have a disaster recovery plan in place to restore data and resume operations quickly after an incident.

10. Cybersecurity Training

Employee Training: Conduct regular cybersecurity training for employees to recognize and respond to security threats1.

Simulated Attacks: Run simulated cyber-attacks to test and improve your organization's response capabilities.

11. Vendor Management

Third-Party Risks: Assess the security practices of vendors and partners to ensure they meet your security standards1.

Contractual Agreements: Include security requirements in contracts with third-party service providers.

12. Incident Response

Response Plan: Develop and regularly update an incident response plan to handle security breaches effectively.

Reporting Mechanisms: Implement clear reporting mechanisms for security incidents to ensure timely action.

By adhering to these best practices, you can significantly enhance your digital security posture and protect yourself and your organization from cyber threats. Remember, security is not a one-time effort but a continuous process that requires vigilance and proactive measures. Stay safe online!

Chapter 7: Integrations and Extensions

Connecting with Other Apps and Services

In today's interconnected digital ecosystem, the ability to connect with other apps and services is a fundamental feature that enhances functionality and user experience. Microsoft Copilot, with its advanced AI capabilities, can integrate with a variety of apps and services to streamline workflows and increase productivity. Here's a detailed exploration of how Copilot facilitates these connections:

1. Integration with Microsoft 365 Suite

Seamless Experience: Copilot is designed to work harmoniously with the Microsoft 365 suite, including Word, Excel, PowerPoint, and Outlook, providing a seamless user experience.

Data Synchronization: It ensures real-time synchronization of data across different applications, enabling a cohesive workflow.

2. Third-Party App Connectivity

API Access: Copilot can connect to third-party apps through APIs, allowing users to extend its capabilities and access a broader range of services.

Single Sign-On: Utilize single sign-on features to connect with third-party services without the need for multiple logins.

3. Enhancing Productivity Tools

Task Automation: Integrate with productivity tools like task managers and calendars to automate scheduling and task tracking.

Custom Workflows: Create custom workflows by connecting Copilot with other services to fit specific business needs.

4. Data Management and Analysis

Database Integration: Connect with databases and storage services to retrieve, analyze, and manage data efficiently.

Analytics Services: Leverage connections with analytics platforms to gain insights and make data-driven decisions.

5. Communication Platforms

Email and Messaging: Integrate with email clients and messaging platforms to streamline communication processes.

Collaboration Tools: Connect with collaboration tools like Microsoft Teams to enhance team coordination and project management.

6. Security and Compliance

Secure Connections: Ensure secure connections with encryption and compliance with industry-standard security protocols.

Privacy Controls: Maintain user privacy by managing permissions and controlling data sharing with connected apps and services.

7. Customization and Flexibility

User-Centric Customization: Tailor connections to suit individual user preferences and requirements for a personalized experience.

Scalability: Adapt the level of connectivity based on the scale of operations, from individual use to enterprise-level integration.

8. Support and Maintenance

Technical Support: Access technical support for troubleshooting issues related to app and service connections.

Regular Updates: Receive updates to maintain compatibility and enhance the integration capabilities of Copilot.

9. Cross-Platform Accessibility

Mobile and Desktop: Ensure Copilot's connectivity features are accessible across both mobile and desktop platforms1.

Cloud Services: Utilize cloud-based services to access Copilot and connected apps from anywhere, at any time.

10. Developer Tools

Extension Development: Use developer tools to create extensions or add-ons that enhance Copilot's connectivity with other apps and services.

Community Contributions: Engage with the developer community to share and access custom integrations1.

By connecting with other apps and services, Microsoft Copilot becomes an even more powerful tool, capable of adapting to a wide range of tasks and workflows. Whether you're looking to automate routine tasks, manage complex projects, or analyze data, Copilot's connectivity features are designed to provide a comprehensive and integrated solution.

Expanding Copilot's Functionality

1. Copilot Pro Subscription

Individual Focus: Copilot Pro is designed for individual users, offering foundational capabilities across devices and apps.

Latest AI Models: Gain priority access to the latest AI models, including OpenAI's GPT-4 Turbo, for enhanced performance.

2. Copilot for Microsoft 365

Organizational Integration: This version is tailored for organizations, providing seamless integration with Microsoft 365 applications.

Custom Copilot GPT: Build your own Copilot GPT with specific skills using the Copilot GPT Builder, coming soon.

3. Extensibility for Developers

Plugins and Connectors: Extend Copilot's skills by transforming your apps into plugins and enriching organizational knowledge with Microsoft Graph connectors.

Custom Skills: Augment Copilot with custom skills specific to your enterprise and users for unique AI scenarios.

4. Copilot Studio

Tailored Experience: Use Copilot Studio to create a pre-customized Copilot tailored for specific topics with simple prompts.

AI Image Creation: Access enhanced AI image creation with Designer for better image quality and format options.

5. Integration with Finance and Operations Apps

Extensibility Tools: Utilize tools to extend and customize the Copilot experience in finance and operations applications.

By leveraging these options, you can enhance Copilot's capabilities to better suit your individual or organizational needs, making it a more powerful tool in your productivity arsenal. Whether it's through a subscription that offers the latest AI advancements or through developer tools that allow for custom integrations, Copilot's functionality can be expanded to meet a wide range of requirements and use cases.

Chapter 8: Customizing Copilot for Various Domains

Tailoring Copilot for Education

Education is a field that constantly evolves, and with the integration of AI technologies like Microsoft Copilot, educators and students are discovering new ways to enhance the learning experience. Here's how Copilot can be tailored for educational purposes:

1. Personalized Learning

Custom Content Creation: Copilot can assist educators in creating personalized content, feedback, and guidance for students, catering to individual learning styles and needs1.

Adaptive Learning Paths: Utilize Copilot to design adaptive learning paths that adjust based on student performance and engagement.

2. Lesson Planning and Resources

Efficient Lesson Planning: Copilot can help educators plan lessons by suggesting activities, resources, and assessments that align with learning objectives1.

Rubric Development: Use Copilot to start or refine rubrics for lessons, ensuring clear and consistent evaluation criteria.

3. Brainstorming and Innovation

Idea Generation: Leverage Copilot to brainstorm new ideas for classroom activities, lesson plans, and supporting materials1.

Creative Assignments: Encourage students to use Copilot for generating creative writing, coding projects, or art concepts.

4. Feedback and Assessment

Drafting Feedback: Copilot can help draft initial feedback for student work, which educators can then personalize and finalize1.

Quick Assessments: Create quizzes and quick assessments with Copilot to gauge student understanding and progress.

5. Research and Inquiry

Information Retrieval: Students and educators can use Copilot to get quick answers to questions without sifting through multiple search results.

Source Evaluation: Copilot provides links to content sources, enabling users to assess the credibility of information.

6. Accessibility and Inclusion

Support for Diverse Needs: Copilot can be used to tailor courses and materials for learners with special needs, ensuring accessibility for all.

Language Translation: Copilot's translation capabilities can help overcome language barriers, making education more inclusive.

7. Professional Development

Educator Training: Teachers can use Copilot for their own professional development, exploring new teaching methodologies and subject matter.

Collaborative Learning: Facilitate professional learning communities where educators share Copilot-generated resources and strategies.

8. Administrative Efficiency

Automating Tasks: Administrative staff can use Copilot to automate routine tasks like scheduling, correspondence, and document management1.

Data Analysis: Analyze educational data with Copilot's assistance to inform decision-making and policy development.

9. Expanding Access

Wider Availability: Copilot is now available to all faculty and higher education students ages 18 and above, with commercial data protection ensuring privacy and security.

Faculty and Staff Eligibility: Copilot for Microsoft 365 eligibility now includes education faculty and staff, expanding the tool's reach within educational institutions.

By tailoring Copilot for education, the potential for enhanced learning and teaching experiences is vast. From creating personalized learning materials to streamlining administrative tasks, Copilot stands as a versatile tool that can transform educational practices.

Leveraging Copilot in Healthcare

The healthcare industry is embracing the power of AI to enhance clinical decision-making, optimize workflows, and improve patient outcomes. Microsoft Copilot, with its advanced AI capabilities, is at the forefront of this transformation. Here's how Copilot is being leveraged in healthcare:

1. Clinical Decision Support

Medical Literature Review: Copilot can sift through the latest medical literature and research, providing clinicians with well-informed and timely information for complex diagnoses.

Treatment Plan Assistance: It assists in creating and evaluating treatment plans by analyzing patient data and suggesting evidence-based recommendations.

2. Administrative Efficiency

Email Assistance: Copilot revolutionizes communication by helping healthcare practitioners craft clear, concise, and professional emails, saving valuable time.

Document Summarization: It excels in summarizing extensive medical reports and documentation, enabling quick extraction of key information.

3. Data Management

Information Extraction: Healthcare professionals can use Copilot to extract relevant information from various reports, converting it into structured data for analysis.

Integration with Excel: The extracted data, including patient details and medical history, can be imported into Excel for further management and study.

4. Workflow Optimization

Task Automation: Copilot automates routine tasks, allowing healthcare staff to focus on patient care and other critical duties2.

Process Streamlining: By driving efficiency within productivity applications, Copilot helps manage the data healthcare professionals don't have time to review manually

5. Enhancing Patient Experience

Personalized Interactions: Copilot facilitates seamless and personalized interactions with patients, contributing to an enhanced overall patient experience.

Patient Education: It can generate patient education materials tailored to individual health conditions and treatment plans.

6. Compliance and Security

Regulatory Compliance: Copilot ensures that all interactions and data handling comply with healthcare regulations such as HIPAA and GDPR.

Secure Data Handling: It maintains the highest standards of data privacy and security, crucial in the sensitive healthcare environment.

7. Professional Development

Continuing Education: Healthcare professionals can use Copilot for their own learning, staying updated with the latest medical advancements and practices.

Training and Simulation: Copilot can assist in creating training modules and simulations for medical education and professional development.

By leveraging Copilot in healthcare, medical professionals can enhance their service delivery, making healthcare more efficient, personalized, and accessible. As AI continues to evolve, its role in supporting the healthcare sector is set to become even more significant, promising a future where technology and healthcare work hand in hand for better patient care.

Copilot for Developers: A Special Focus

Developers are at the heart of innovation, and with the advent of AI tools like Microsoft Copilot, their workflow and productivity have been significantly transformed. Here's a detailed guide on how Copilot is specially focused on aiding developers:

1. AI-Powered Coding Assistance

Real-Time Suggestions: Copilot provides real-time coding suggestions, helping developers write code more efficiently and with fewer errors.

Strategic Focus: It allows developers to concentrate on strategic aspects of coding by handling routine tasks.

2. Integration with Development Tools

Visual Studio Code: Copilot integrates with popular development environments like Visual Studio Code, enhancing the coding experience.

GitHub Integration: It seamlessly works with GitHub, offering suggestions based on the vast repository of code available on the platform.

3. Customization and Extensibility

Copilot Extensions: Developers can build Copilot extensions to extend its functionality within Microsoft 365, using tools like Azure AI Services.

Personalized Experience: Create custom Copilots tailored to specific functions or roles within an organization.

4. Enhanced Developer Productivity

Automated Code Review: Copilot can assist in code reviews by suggesting improvements and identifying potential issues.

Code Refactoring: It aids in refactoring code, ensuring that the codebase is clean, maintainable, and adheres to best practices.

5. Learning and Skill Development

Continuous Learning: Copilot serves as a learning tool, helping developers stay updated with the latest coding practices and languages.

Interactive Tutorials: Access interactive tutorials and documentation to enhance coding skills and knowledge.

6. Collaboration and Teamwork

Team Copilot: Utilize Team Copilot for collaborative coding, allowing teams to work together more effectively.

Shared Knowledge: Share insights and solutions across teams, fostering a collaborative environment for development.

7. Support for Multiple Languages

Multilingual Coding: Copilot supports a wide range of programming languages, making it a versatile tool for developers working in different tech stacks.

8. Streamlining Development Workflows

Workflow Optimization: Copilot optimizes development workflows by automating repetitive tasks and providing intelligent suggestions.

DevOps Integration: Integrate with DevOps tools to streamline the software development lifecycle.

9. Building on the Copilot Stack

Copilot Stack: Leverage the Copilot Stack, which includes the Windows Copilot Runtime, to run AI applications locally and enhance Windows applications with AI features.

Copilot Library: Access a library of models and APIs to integrate AI into applications, with support for PyTorch running natively on Windows.

10. Future of AI in Development

Innovative Solutions: Explore innovative solutions across the Microsoft Cloud with Copilot, shaping the future of software development.

AI-Driven Development: Embrace the shift towards AI-driven development, where Copilot plays a crucial role in enhancing developer capabilities.

Microsoft Copilot is not just a coding assistant; it's a partner for developers, providing a platform to innovate, publish, and monetize faster. With its focus on developers, Copilot is set to redefine the software development landscape, making it more efficient, collaborative, and innovative.

Chapter 9: The Future of AI Assistants

Predictions and Possibilities

The realm of AI and technology is rapidly evolving, with new advancements reshaping our world and opening up a myriad of possibilities. Below is a detailed look at the predictions and possibilities that are on the horizon for AI and technology:

1. Generative AI Expansion

Customized Chatbots: Generative AI will continue to grow, with an emphasis on user-friendly platforms that allow people to customize powerful language models and create their own mini chatbots1.

Multimodal Capabilities: State-of-the-art AI models will become increasingly multimodal, processing not just text but also images and videos, unlocking new applications.

2. AI in Business and Creative Workflows

Business Integration: Companies will increasingly embrace AI across creative workflows, integrating AI solutions into everyday business operations.

Creative Industries: AI will play a significant role in creative industries, aiding in everything from graphic design to content creation.

3. Healthcare Transformation

Drug Development: AI in healthcare will propel drug development and personalized medicine, leading to more targeted and effective treatments.

Clinical Support: AI will provide clinicians with advanced decision support tools, enhancing diagnostic accuracy and patient care.

4. Responsible AI and Ethics

Ethical Focus: There will be a greater emphasis on responsible AI, with efforts to address issues of bias, privacy, and ethical use of technology.

Regulatory Developments: Policymakers will introduce regulations to govern the use of AI, ensuring it aligns with societal values and norms.

5. Customer Interaction Redefined

AI Customer Service: AI will redefine how businesses interact with their customers, offering more personalized and efficient customer service experiences.

Virtual Agents: More powerful virtual agents will emerge, capable of handling complex customer interactions with ease.

6. Open Source and Accessibility

Open Source AI: The open-source AI movement will continue to thrive, providing accessible AI tools and resources to a broader audience.

Local Models and Data Pipelines: Customized local models and data pipelines will become more prevalent, allowing for greater control over AI applications.

7. AI in Everyday Life

Domestic AI: AI will become more integrated into our daily lives, with smart home devices and personal assistants becoming more advanced and ubiquitous.

Education and Learning: AI will transform education, providing personalized learning experiences and supporting educators in curriculum development.

8. Technological Convergence

Interdisciplinary Innovation: AI will converge with other technologies like blockchain, IoT, and quantum computing, leading to interdisciplinary innovations.

Sustainable AI: Efforts will be made to make AI more sustainable, focusing on energy-efficient models and environmentally friendly practices.

These predictions paint a picture of a future where AI is not just a tool but an integral part of our lives, driving innovation, efficiency, and growth across various sectors. As we navigate this future, it's crucial to balance the potential of AI with considerations for its responsible use, ensuring that the technology benefits society as a whole.

Ethical Considerations and Debates

Ethical considerations in research are critical to maintaining the integrity of the scientific process and protecting the rights and welfare of participants. Here's a overview of the key ethical considerations and debates in research:

1. Voluntary Participation

Autonomy: Participants should voluntarily consent to be part of a study without coercion or undue influence.

Freedom to Withdraw: They must have the right to withdraw from the study at any point without penalty.

2. Informed Consent

Full Disclosure: Researchers must provide all relevant information about the study, including its purpose, procedures, risks, and benefits.

Comprehension: Participants should understand the information provided and consent must be obtained before the study begins.

3. Anonymity and Confidentiality

Protecting Identity: Researchers should protect the identity of participants, ensuring that personal information is not disclosed without consent.

Data Security: Measures must be in place to secure data and maintain confidentiality.

4. Minimizing Harm

Risk Assessment: Researchers should minimize potential risks to participants, including physical, psychological, and social harm.

Beneficence: The benefits of research should outweigh any potential risks to the participants.

5. Results Communication

Transparency: Findings should be communicated honestly and openly, without fabrication, falsification, or misrepresentation.

Feedback to Participants: Researchers should provide feedback to participants about the study's results when appropriate.

6. Respect for Persons

Individual Rights: Research should respect the dignity, rights, and values of individuals, recognizing their autonomy and decision-making capabilities.

Vulnerable Populations: Special considerations should be given to vulnerable groups who may have limited capacity to give informed consent.

7. Justice

Fair Treatment: The selection of research participants should be fair, and the benefits and burdens of research should be distributed equitably.

Access to Benefits: Participants should have access to the benefits resulting from the research, such as new treatments or interventions.

8. Scientific Integrity

Rigorous Methodology: Research should be designed and conducted rigorously to ensure the validity and reliability of the results.

Peer Review: Studies should undergo peer review to evaluate the quality and ethical standards of the research.

9. Debates and Challenges

Ethical Dilemmas: Researchers often face ethical dilemmas where they must balance competing values and interests.

Evolving Standards: Ethical standards in research are not static and evolve over time, leading to ongoing debates about best practices.

10. Regulatory Compliance

Institutional Review Boards (IRBs): Research involving human participants typically requires review and approval by an IRB to ensure ethical standards are met.

Legal Requirements: Researchers must comply with all applicable laws and regulations governing research ethics.

Ethical considerations in research are fundamental to the trustworthiness of the scientific enterprise and the societal acceptance of research findings. As the field of research ethics continues to evolve, ongoing dialogue and debate are essential to address emerging ethical issues and challenges.

Staying Informed on AI Developments

Staying informed on AI developments is crucial for anyone interested in the field, whether you're a professional, a student, or simply an enthusiast. The pace at which AI is evolving means that new breakthroughs, applications, and ethical considerations are emerging regularly. Here's a guide to help you stay updated with the latest in AI:

Understanding AI Domains and Applications

AI is not a monolithic field; it encompasses various domains and applications, each with its own set of developments:

GPT-3: An advanced language model that has revolutionized natural language processing.

Computer Vision: This involves visual data analysis and has applications ranging from medical diagnostics to autonomous vehicles.

Reinforcement Learning: A type of machine learning based on reward-based training, crucial for developing systems that learn complex behaviors.

Transfer Learning: This allows for knowledge reuse across different AI tasks, making machine learning models more efficient.

Biometrics: Used for identity verification, this has significant implications for security and privacy.

AI in Healthcare: Personalized medicine is one of the promising applications of AI in healthcare, offering tailored treatment plans1.

Explainable AI: There's a growing demand for transparent AI systems that provide insights into their decision-making processes.

AI-assisted Creativity: AI is being used for artistic expression and collaboration, opening new avenues for creators.

Virtual Agents: Intelligent interaction with virtual agents is becoming more sophisticated, enhancing customer service experiences.

AI-optimized Hardware: Specialized hardware architectures are being developed to better support AI computations.

Keeping Up with the News

Following reputable news sources and technology blogs can provide insights into the latest AI developments:

Forbes Tech Council discusses how applied technology like GenAI and AR are transforming user experiences.

Texas Standard shares updates on the latest AI developments, including insights from tech experts.

MIT News covers a wide range of AI topics, from new methods in video analysis to advancements in AI-based material property adjustments.

Engaging with the Community

Participating in forums, attending conferences, and joining

 AI-focused groups can help you network with peers and stay informed:

Online Forums: Platforms like Reddit, Stack Overflow, and specialized AI forums are great for discussions and knowledge exchange.

Conferences: Events like NeurIPS, ICML, and CVPR are where many new research papers and technologies are presented.

Meetups and Workshops: Local meetups and workshops can provide hands-on experience and direct interaction with AI professionals.

Educational Resources

Educational platforms offer courses and materials to deepen your understanding of AI:

MOOCs: Websites like Coursera, edX, and Udacity offer courses on AI from top universities and companies.

Research Papers: Staying current with the latest research papers on arXiv or through academic journals can be invaluable.

Books: Reading books from AI thought leaders and researchers can provide deeper insights into where the field is headed.

Ethical Considerations

As AI continues to advance, ethical considerations become increasingly important:

Bias and Fairness: Understanding how bias can enter AI systems and ways to mitigate it is crucial.

Privacy: With AI's ability to process vast amounts of data, privacy concerns must be addressed.

Regulation: Keeping an eye on how governments and international bodies regulate AI is important for anticipating changes in the field.

By following these steps, you can stay informed on AI developments and be part of the conversation shaping the future of this transformative technology.

Chapter 10: Appendices

Glossary of Terms

Microsoft Copilot Glossary of Terms

Copilot: Natural language assistants that help with creative tasks, generate insights, execute automated workflows, and more.

Custom Copilot: A tailored version of Microsoft Copilot that combines specific instructions, additional knowledge, and a mix of skills.

Azure OpenAI Service: An API service that enables developers to query OpenAI's language models with Microsoft's reliability guarantees.

Azure AI Studio: A pro-code development platform for full customization and control over AI applications and models.

Microsoft Copilot: An accessible AI interface that integrates with Microsoft products to enhance user experience and productivity.

Microsoft Copilot Studio: A tool for integrating AI into Microsoft 365 or Power Platform products, offering prebuilt and custom AI models.

Copilot Extensions: Enhancements that customize Microsoft Copilot with new actions and knowledge specific to the user's daily workflows.

Plugins: A type of Copilot extension that can be written once and run on any Copilot surface.

Microsoft Copilot Connectors: Extensions for low/no code experiences, bundling capabilities from various Microsoft services.

Microsoft Graph Connectors: Index data from various sources into Microsoft Graph to augment capabilities of services like Microsoft Copilot.

Power Platform Connectors: Enable interaction with external data sources and services for the Microsoft Power Platform.

Teams Message Extension: A Microsoft Teams feature that allows users to interact with web services through Adaptive Cards.

Frequently Asked Questions

Frequently Asked Questions about Microsoft Copilot

What can Microsoft 365 Copilot do?

Microsoft 365 Copilot can assist with a variety of tasks, including drafting emails, creating documents, generating code, and more. It leverages advanced AI to understand context and provide relevant suggestions.

How does Copilot work?

Copilot works by using language models to interpret user input and generate appropriate responses or content. It integrates with Microsoft products to enhance productivity and creativity.

How do I best use Copilot?

To best use Copilot, clearly state your request or question, and provide context if necessary. Copilot can help with creative writing, summarizing information, coding, and even answering questions based on its knowledge.

Can I trust that Copilot's answers are always accurate?

While Copilot aims to provide accurate information, it's always good practice to verify the answers, especially for critical tasks. Copilot's knowledge is up-to-date until 2021, and it uses web search for the latest information.

How is the quality of Copilot's responses evaluated?

The quality of Copilot's responses is continually assessed through user feedback and internal testing to ensure reliability and relevance.

Do I need to link my personal Microsoft account to my work account to use Copilot?

No, you do not need to link your personal Microsoft account to your work account to use Copilot. However, doing so may enhance the personalized experience.

Can I use Copilot with my work account and personal account at the same time?

Yes, Copilot can be used with both your work and personal accounts, depending on the settings and permissions set by your organization.

Where can I learn more about privacy for Microsoft 365 Copilot?

You can learn more about privacy for Microsoft 365 Copilot by visiting the official Microsoft support page.

Where can I learn more about Microsoft's commitment to Responsible AI?

Microsoft's commitment to Responsible AI can be explored in detail on their official website, which outlines principles and practices.

How will Microsoft 365 Copilot handle and protect my sensitive data and information?

Microsoft 365 Copilot is designed with security and privacy in mind, adhering to Microsoft's strict data protection policies to safeguard sensitive data and information.

11. About the Author

My name is (-----)As an enthusiast of Microsoft Copilot with a decade of experience in the tech industry, I've had the privilege of witnessing and contributing to the remarkable evolution of AI and its integration into our daily lives. My journey began with a fascination for the potential of AI to transform how we interact with technology, and over the years, I've dedicated myself to exploring and understanding the depths of this field.

Throughout my career, I've authored several articles and books that delve into the intricacies of AI, focusing on how tools like Microsoft Copilot can enhance productivity, creativity, and decision-making. My work aims to demystify AI for a broader audience, breaking down complex concepts into accessible insights.

My passion for technology extends beyond writing; I actively participate in forums, workshops, and conferences, engaging with a community of like-minded individuals who share a vision for the future of AI. This engagement has not only enriched my knowledge but also allowed me to contribute to the discourse on ethical AI use and privacy considerations.

As an author, I strive to provide readers with practical guides and thought-provoking discussions on the latest AI trends and developments. Whether it's exploring hidden features of Copilot or examining the ethical implications of AI, my goal is to equip readers with the knowledge they need to navigate the ever-evolving tech landscape confidently.

In my latest book, I offer a comprehensive look at Microsoft Copilot, detailing its capabilities, best practices, and tips for maximizing its potential. I believe that AI, when used responsibly, can be a powerful ally in our quest for innovation and efficiency. It's an exciting time to be at the forefront of this technological revolution, and I'm eager to see what the next decade holds for Microsoft Copilot and the world of AI.

CONCLUSION

In conclusion, the Microsoft Copilot User Guide serves as a beacon for navigating the vast and dynamic landscape of AI-assisted productivity. Throughout this guide, we have explored the multifaceted capabilities of Copilot, from its seamless integration with Microsoft products to its advanced features that cater to a wide array of professional and creative needs.

We delved into the setup and customization options that allow users to tailor Copilot to their unique workflows, ensuring an optimized and personal experience. The guide also highlighted the importance of staying informed on AI developments, ethical considerations, and privacy practices, emphasizing Microsoft's commitment to responsible AI use.

As we close this chapter, it's clear that Microsoft Copilot is more than just a tool; it's a companion that evolves with you, learning from your patterns and preferences to become an indispensable part of your daily routine. Whether you're drafting documents, coding, or seeking creative inspiration, Copilot stands ready to assist with intelligence and intuition.

The journey with Microsoft Copilot is one of continuous learning and discovery. With each update and new feature, Copilot redefines the boundaries of what's possible, empowering users to achieve more with less effort. As you harness the power of Copilot, remember that the true potential of AI lies in the synergy between human creativity and machine intelligence.

Embrace the future with Microsoft Copilot, and let it elevate your ambitions to new heights. Here's to the next chapter of innovation, efficiency, and collaboration. Happy piloting!

Thank you note

Dear Esteemed Reader,

As the journey of crafting the "Microsoft Copilot User Guide" comes to a close, I find myself reflecting on the path we've traversed together. Your support as a reader and buyer of this book is not just a commercial transaction; it's a shared commitment to the pursuit of knowledge and the empowerment that comes with it.

I extend my heartfelt thanks to you for choosing to embark on this exploration of Microsoft Copilot's capabilities. Your engagement is what transforms these pages from mere words to a conduit of innovation and productivity. It is my sincere hope that this guide serves as a valuable resource, illuminating the features and possibilities that Copilot offers.

Your trust in this work reaffirms the importance of creating comprehensive, user-friendly guides in the ever-evolving landscape of technology. As you apply the insights from this book, may you find Copilot to be an ally in your professional endeavors and a spark for your creativity.

Thank you for your patronage, and more importantly, for your curiosity and willingness to learn. May our paths cross again in the future volumes and updates that continue to demystify the world of artificial intelligence.

With gratitude,

[Your Name]

Author & Microsoft Copilot Enthusiast

Questions

1. What feature of Microsoft Copilot do you find most beneficial for your daily tasks?

_____

_____

_____

_____

2. How has Microsoft Copilot changed the way you approach problem-solving in your work?

_____

_____

_____

_____

3. Can you share an instance where Microsoft Copilot significantly improved your productivity?

_____

_____

_____

_____

4. What was the most surprising thing you learned about AI from the guide?

_____

_____

_____

_____

5. How do you plan to implement the ethical considerations discussed in the guide in your use of AI?

_____

_____

_____

_____

6. Which customization option of Microsoft Copilot do you think will be most useful for you, and why?

_____

_____

_____

_____

7. What is one hidden feature of Microsoft Copilot that you hadn't known about before reading this guide?

_____

_____

_____

_____

8. How comfortable do you feel with the privacy measures in place for Microsoft Copilot after reading the guide?

_____

_____

_____

_____

9. What is one way you believe Microsoft Copilot could be improved based on your understanding from the guide?

_____

_____

_____

_____

10. How do you envision AI tools like Microsoft Copilot evolving in the next five years?

_____

_____

_____

_____

11. What steps will you take to stay informed about future developments of Microsoft Copilot?

_____

_____

_____

_____

12. How has the guide influenced your perception of AI's role in the workplace?

_____

_____

_____

_____

13. What advice would you give to a new user of Microsoft Copilot based on insights from the guide?

_____

_____

_____

_____

14. Which section of the guide did you find most challenging, and how did you overcome it?

_____

_____

_____

_____

15. How has the guide helped you in understanding the importance of AI literacy?

_____

_____

_____

_____

16. In what ways do you think Microsoft Copilot can contribute to creative endeavors?

_____

_____

_____

_____

17. What ethical dilemma related to AI use do you find most compelling, and how does the guide address it?

_____

_____

_____

_____

18. How do you plan to use the troubleshooting tips provided in the guide?

_____

_____

_____

_____

19. What is one question you still have after reading the guide?

_____

_____

_____

_____

20. How likely are you to recommend the "Microsoft Copilot User Guide" to others, and why?

_____

_____

_____

_____